Dinos

Origami

This edition published in the United Kingdom in 2015 by
Collins & Brown
1 Gower Street
London
WC1E 6HD

An imprint of Pavilion Books Company Ltd

The paper sheets in this book can be used to make the following projects
Dimetrodon, Protoceratops and Coelophysis.

The origami dinosaurs in this book live in a fictional world that is not
intended to be representative of the Prehistoric era.

ISBN 978-1-910232-26-2

A CIP catalogue for this book is available from the British Library.

10 9 8 7 6 5 4 3 2 1

Reproduction by Mission, Hong Kong
Printed and bound by 1010 Printing International Ltd, China

This book can be ordered direct from the publisher at
www.pavilionbooks.com

Dinosaur
Origami

20 Prehistoric origami projects with paper sheets to get you started

Fernando Gilgado Gómez

COLLINS & BROWN

CONTENTS

SYMBOLS

Valley fold	– – – – – – –	
Mountain fold	— · — · — · —	
Fold on dotted line	————	
X-ray view showing detail at back	··················	
Fold forwards		
Fold under		
Fold and unfold		

Turn the paper over/repeat on other side		
Rotate the paper		
Fold steps, open out		
Fold steps, flatten and bend		
Enlarged detail		
Open view		
Sink fold		
Open out and flatten (squash fold)		

DINOLINE

MILLION YEARS AGO	AGES	PERIODS
50	MESOZOIC	CRETACEOUS
100	MESOZOIC	CRETACEOUS
150	MESOZOIC	JURASSIC
200		TRIASSIC
250		PERMIAN
300		CARBONIFEROUS
350	PALEOZOIC	DEVONIAN
400	PALEOZOIC	SILURIAN
450		ORDOVICIAN
500		CAMBRIAN
550		CAMBRIAN
600	PRECAMBRIAN	PRECAMBRIAN
2500	PRECAMBRIAN	PRECAMBRIAN

ORIGAMISAURUS

Each dinosaur comes with its own classification box. This helpfully breaks down the vital dinostats so you have all the information you need before you start the project.

CLASSIFICATION

MEANING: Three-Horned Face
DIETARY PREFERENCE: Herbivore
PERIOD: Jurassic
SKILL LEVEL:

PAPER SIZE: 20cm x 20cm (8in x 8in)
MODEL SIZE: 10cm (4in)

Before you start folding your dinosaur, read through our helpful hints:

1. First of all, note the skill level:

= Beginner

= Moderate

= Advanced

2. Follow each step in order without skipping any stages. A fold might look irrelevant, but it may be the foundation to a later, more complex fold.

3. Before folding the step, it can help to look at the following step, which will show the next stage.

4. Try practising on a piece of scrap paper first to iron out any problems.

5. Most importantly, enjoy making each project – we did!

CLASSIFICATION

NAME'S MEANING: Jurassic Fern
DIETARY PREFERENCE: None
PERIOD: Jurassic
SKILL LEVEL:

PAPER SIZE: 20cm x 20cm (8in x 8in)
MODEL SIZE: 3.5cm (4in)

PREHISTORIC FERN

Providing a rich habitat for our friendly herbivores, this prehistoric fern crops up all over Dinoworld. Try making these using a lush green paper for a natural look. You can adjust the paper size to make a larger version, too.

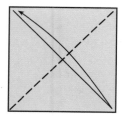

1. Fold and unfold

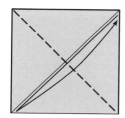

2. Fold and unfold

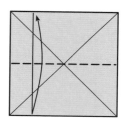

3. Fold and unfold

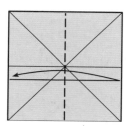

4. Fold and unfold

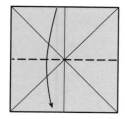

5. Fold in half

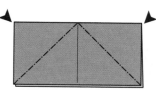

6. Push in to the dotted line

7. Fold on the dotted line

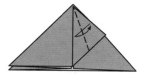

8. Fold and unfold

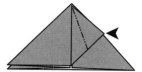

9. Push in

10. Fold up

11. Fold and unfold

12. Push in

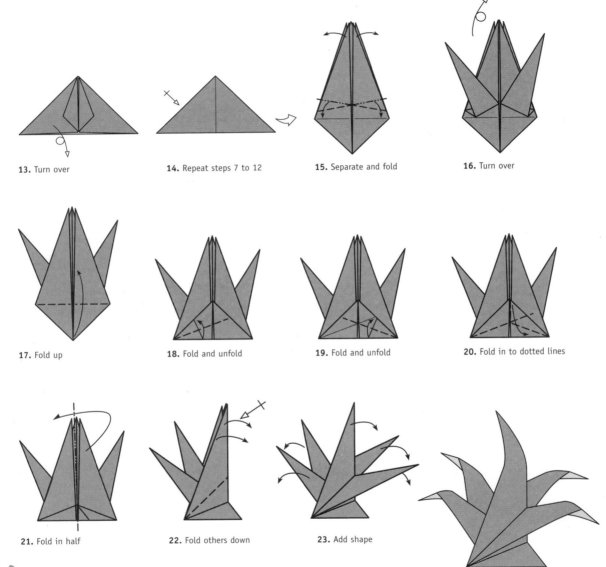

13. Turn over

14. Repeat steps 7 to 12

15. Separate and fold

16. Turn over

17. Fold up

18. Fold and unfold

19. Fold and unfold

20. Fold in to dotted lines

21. Fold in half

22. Fold others down

23. Add shape

VOLCANO

This bubbling magma chamber awaits patiently for the right moment to erupt once more over Dinoworld. Try filling the cavity with scraps of red material for a realistic look. Simple and quick to make, this is a perfect project for a speedy result.

CLASSIFICATION

MEANING: Molten Vent
DIETARY PREFERENCE: None
PERIOD: All
SKILL LEVEL:

PAPER SIZE: 50cm x 50cm (18in x 18in)
MODEL SIZE: 23cm (9in)

1. Fold and unfold

2. Fold and unfold

3. Fold and unfold

4. Fold and unfold

A

B　　　　　C

D

5. Join the corners A, B and C with D

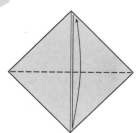

6. Fold and unfold

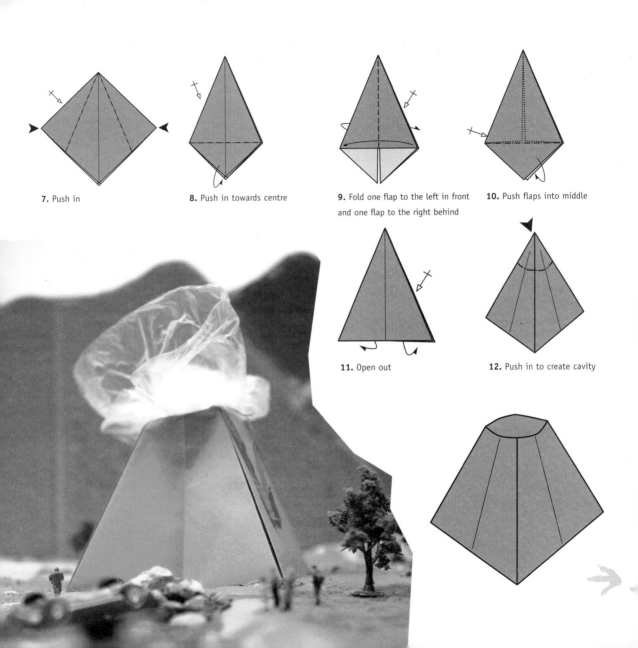

7. Push in

8. Push in towards centre

9. Fold one flap to the left in front and one flap to the right behind

10. Push flaps into middle

11. Open out

12. Push in to create cavity

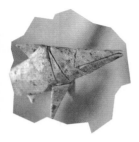

ICHTHYOSAURUS

Sharp teeth, long jaws and a shark-like dorsal fin make him a fearsome character. Living in the ocean, he enjoys a diet of fish, octopus and any sea dweller he can get his pearly whites into. Hobbies include diving and other watersports.

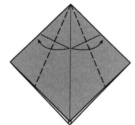

1. Join the corners A, B and C with D

2. Fold and unfold

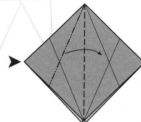

3. Fold and unfold

4. Press in and flatten

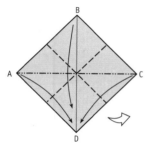

5. Fold in and fold up

6. Fold piece down

7. Fold piece over

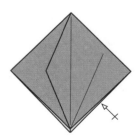

8. Repeat steps 4 to 7 symmetrically

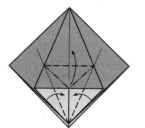

CLASSIFICATION

MEANING: Lizard Fish
DIETARY PREFERENCE: Carnivore
PERIOD: Cretaceous
SKILL LEVEL:

PAPER SIZE: 21cm x 21cm (8¼in x 8¼in)
MODEL SIZE: 10cm (4in)

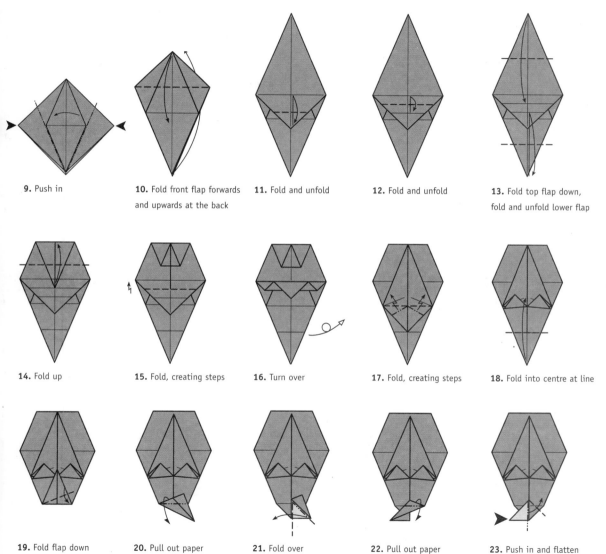

9. Push in

10. Fold front flap forwards and upwards at the back

11. Fold and unfold

12. Fold and unfold

13. Fold top flap down, fold and unfold lower flap

14. Fold up

15. Fold, creating steps

16. Turn over

17. Fold, creating steps

18. Fold into centre at line

19. Fold flap down

20. Pull out paper

21. Fold over

22. Pull out paper

23. Push in and flatten

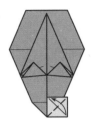

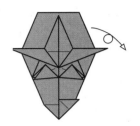

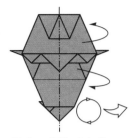

24. Fold and unfold

25. Fold out flaps

26. Turn over

27. Turn, folding in half

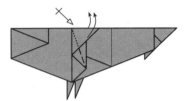

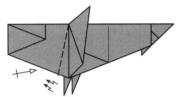

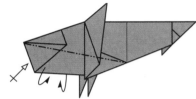

28. Stretch upwards

29. Fold, creating the steps

30. Fold under

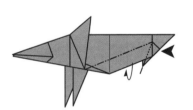

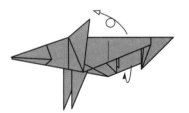

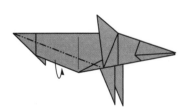

31. Fold under

32. Turn over

33. Fold under

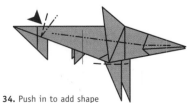

34. Push in to add shape

DINOSAUR BABY

Newly hatched and eagerly awaiting his parent's homecoming, this little nipper needs a good meal. Living high up in the clifftops and safely tucked away from any predators, he's got a magnificent view of the dinoscape.

1. Fold and unfold

2. Join the side to the circled point

CLASSIFICATION

NAME'S MEANING: Newborn dinosaur
DIETARY PREFERENCE: Carnivore
PERIOD: Any
SKILL LEVEL:

PAPER SIZE: 21cm x 21cm (8¼in x 8¼in)
MODEL SIZE: 11cm (4¼in)

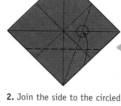

3. Fold and unfold

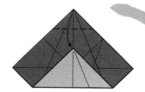

4. Fold into centre

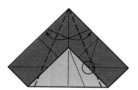

5. Fold into centre

6. See close-ups in steps 7 and 8

7. Push in and fold

8. Finished section

9. Turn over

10. Fold into centre

11. Fold and unfold

12. Fold and unfold

13. Fold and unfold

14. Fold pieces in

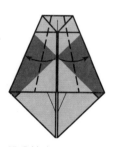

15. Fold pieces out

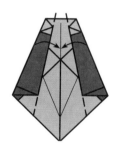

16. Fold pieces in

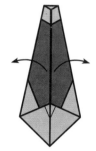

17. Unfold

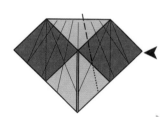

18. Push in

19. Push in

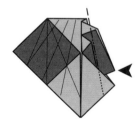

20. Push in

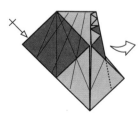

21. Repeat steps 18 to 20 symmetrically

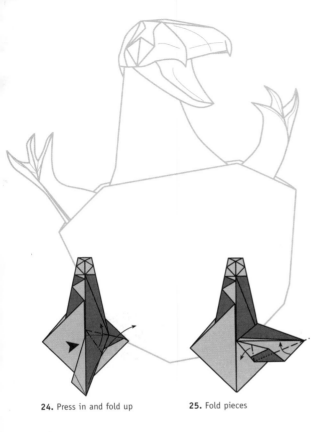

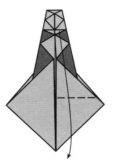

22. Fold piece down

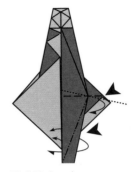

23. Fold pieces in

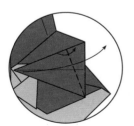

24. Press in and fold up

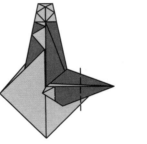

25. Fold pieces

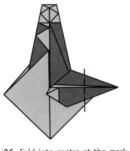

26. Fold into centre at the mark

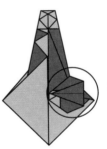

27. See close-ups in steps 28 to 40

28. Fold at mark

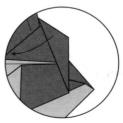

29. Fold at mark

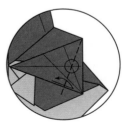

30. Stretch

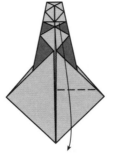

31. Fold and unfold

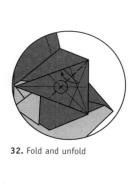

32. Fold and unfold

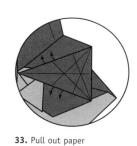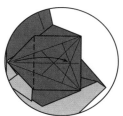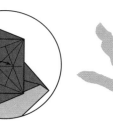

33. Pull out paper

34. Fold at mark

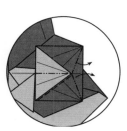

35. Fold at mark

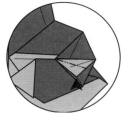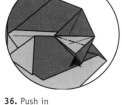

36. Push in

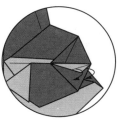

37. Unfold the joined paper

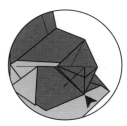

38. Push in

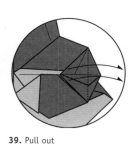

39. Pull out

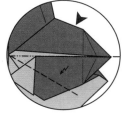

40. Fold steps and push in

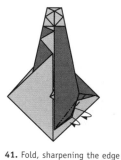

41. Fold, sharpening the edge

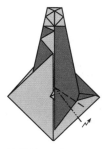

42. Fold, creating steps

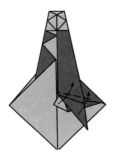

43. Fold up

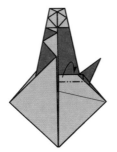

44. Fold back

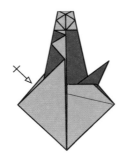

45. Repeat steps 22 to 44 symmetrically

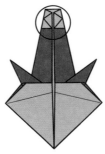

46. See close-ups in steps 47 to 50

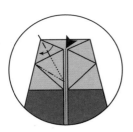

47. Push in

48. Fold and unfold

49. Press in and flatten

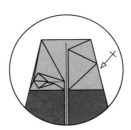

50. Repeat steps 47 to 49 symmetrically

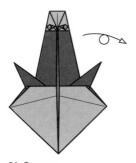

51. Turn over

52. See close-ups in steps 53 to 55

53. Fold out

54. Push in

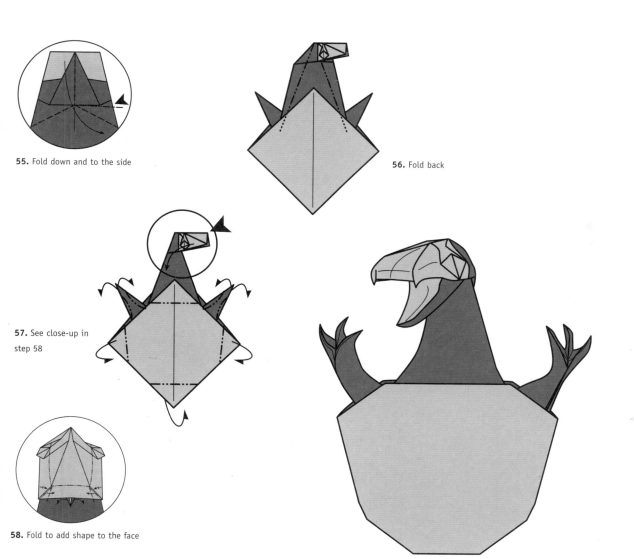

55. Fold down and to the side

56. Fold back

57. See close-up in step 58

58. Fold to add shape to the face

DIMETRODON

Don't let appearances deceive you. This pint-sized reptile may be short on stature but sharp canines and shearing teeth make him a thick-skinned and cold-blooded predator. Interestingly enough, the Dimetrodon is not actually a dinosaur, but in fact, classified as a pelycosaur.

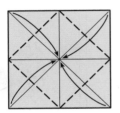

1. Fold in the corners

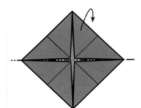

2. Fold in half

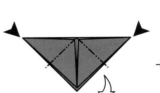

3. Push in

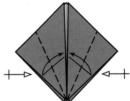

4. Fold and unfold

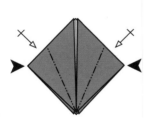

5. Push in

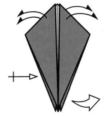

6. Open out the four flaps

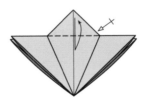

7. Fold and unfold

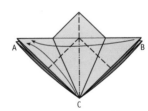

8. Join corners B and C with A

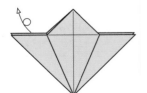

9. Turn over

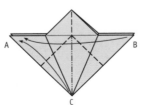

10. Join corners B and C with A

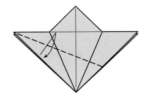

11. Fold and unfold

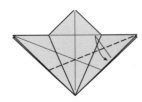

12. Fold and unfold

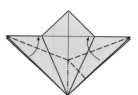

13. Fold up

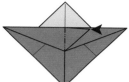

14. Push in

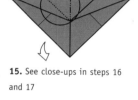

15. See close-ups in steps 16 and 17

16. Fold down

17. Finished fold

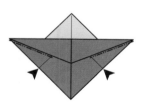

18. Push in

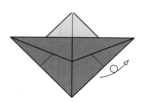

19. Turn over

CLASSIFICATION

NAME'S MEANING: Two types of teeth
DIETARY PREFERENCE: Carnivore
PERIOD: Permian
SKILL LEVEL:

PAPER SIZE: 15cm x 15cm (6in x 6in)
MODEL SIZE: 9cm (3½in)

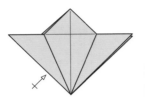

20. Repeat steps 11 to 17

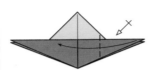

21. Fold in

22. Fold up

23. Fold down

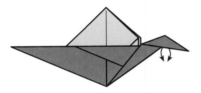

24. Pull out paper

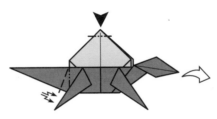

25. Fold back

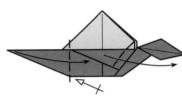

25. Fold pieces over, creating front leg

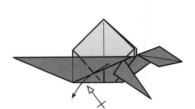

26. Fold down, creating back leg

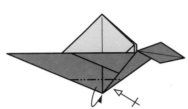

27. Push in, fold steps to create feet

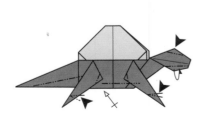

28. Add shape

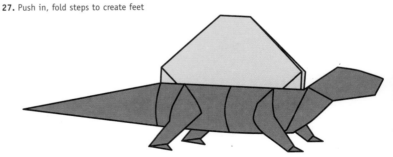

PALM TREE

Giving the landscape its tropical look, the palm tree is a hardy addition. Boasting large, weeping leaves, it can cope with extreme weather, temperatures and conditions. They're easy to make so group them together for an authentic prehistoric jungle.

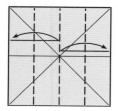

1. Fold and unfold

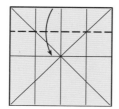

2. Fold

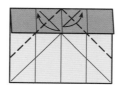

3. Fold and unfold

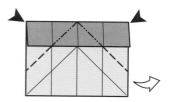

4. Push in

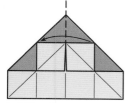

5. Fold section in half

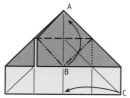

6. Join A and B, folding into centre with C

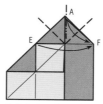

7. Join A and E with F

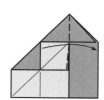

8. Fold over

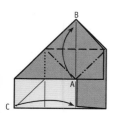

9. Join A and B, folding into centre with C

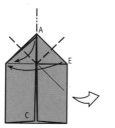

10. Join A and E, folding C into centre

11. Press in sections at the front and back

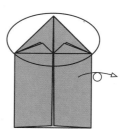

12. Finished fold

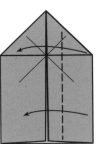

13. Fold on line

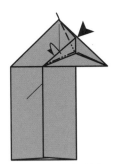

14. Push in and fold down

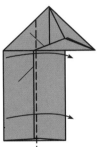

15. Fold panel over

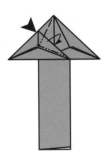

16. Push in and fold down

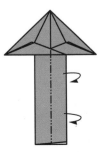

17. Fold back

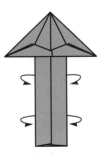

18. Pull out paper

CLASSIFICATION

NAME'S MEANING: Unbranched Trunk
DIETARY PREFERENCE: None
PERIOD: Any
SKILL LEVEL:

PAPER SIZE: 30cm x 30cm (12in x 12in)
MODEL SIZE: 16cm (6in)

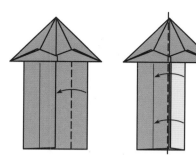  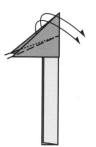 

19. Fold in   **20.** Fold in   **21.** Fold into centre   **22.** Fold over top   **23.** Press in

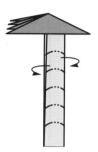  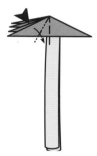

24. Give shape   **25.** Press in and flatten

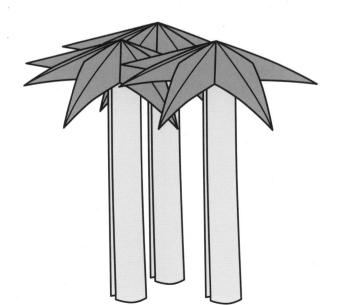

26. Repeat, forming leaves

BRACHIOSAURUS

One of the largest animals to ever walk the Earth and weighing up to 78 tonnes, this colossal beast cannot be missed. A long neck and a giraffe-like stance make reaching the best leaves at the tops of the trees a breeze. Don't be afraid, he's a gentle giant and prefers plants to human flesh.

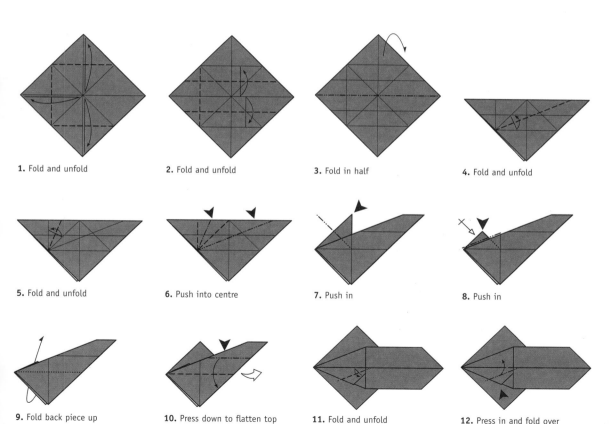

1. Fold and unfold

2. Fold and unfold

3. Fold in half

4. Fold and unfold

5. Fold and unfold

6. Push into centre

7. Push in

8. Push in

9. Fold back piece up

10. Press down to flatten top

11. Fold and unfold

12. Press in and fold over

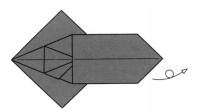

13. Turn over

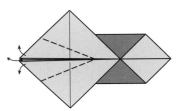

14. Open and stretch

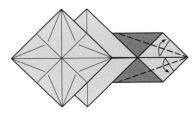

15. Fold and unfold

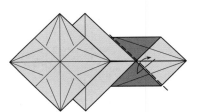

16. Fold and unfold

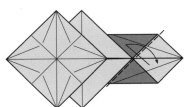

17. Fold and unfold

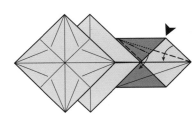

18. Push in and fold over

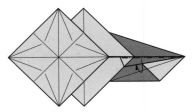

19. Fold under

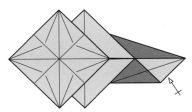

20. Repeat steps 18 to 19 symmetrically

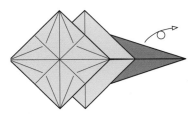

21. Turn over

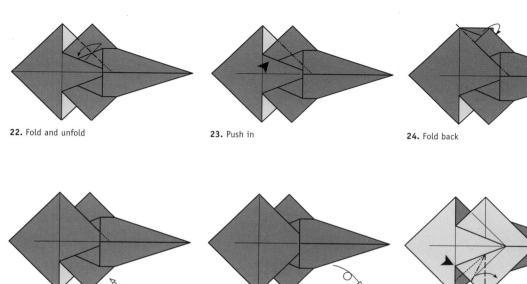

22. Fold and unfold

23. Push in

24. Fold back

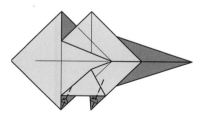

25. Repeat steps 22 to 24 symmetrically

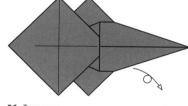

26. Turn over

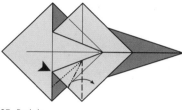

27. Push in

28. Fold and unfold

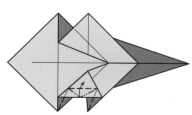

29. Stretch

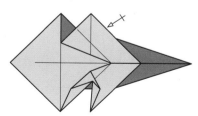

30. Repeat steps 27 to 29 symmetrically

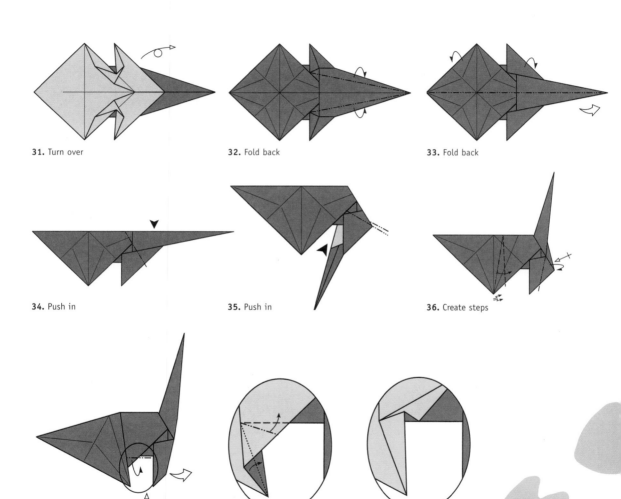

31. Turn over

32. Fold back

33. Fold back

34. Push in

35. Push in

36. Create steps

37. See close-up in steps 38 to 39

38. Fold in and up

39. Finished view of fold

40. Create steps

41. Push in

42. Fold in

43. Give shape

44. Shape head

45. Fold head

46. Finished view

PARASAUROLOPHUS

With its short narrow snout, pebbly skin and pointy tail, this harmless dinosaur had no natural defences. But it did make a noise like a foghorn, meaning you are more likely to hear it rather than see it coming!

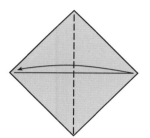

1. Fold and unfold

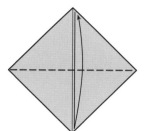

2. Fold and unfold

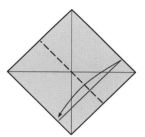

3. Fold and unfold

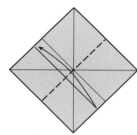

4. Fold and unfold

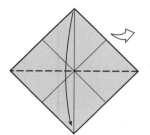

5. Fold in half

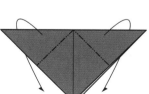

6. Fold corners down

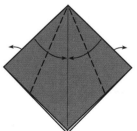

7. Fold centre flaps in and fold out flaps behind

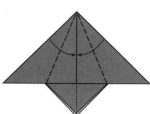

8. Fold into centre

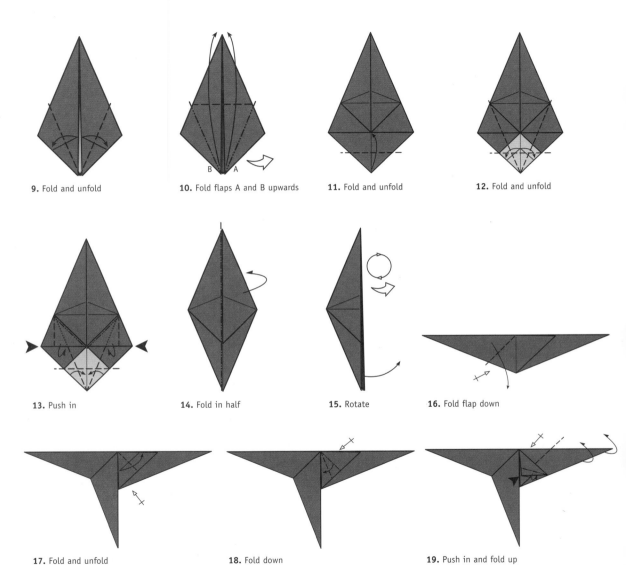

9. Fold and unfold

10. Fold flaps A and B upwards

B   A

11. Fold and unfold

12. Fold and unfold

13. Push in

14. Fold in half

15. Rotate

16. Fold flap down

17. Fold and unfold

18. Fold down

19. Push in and fold up

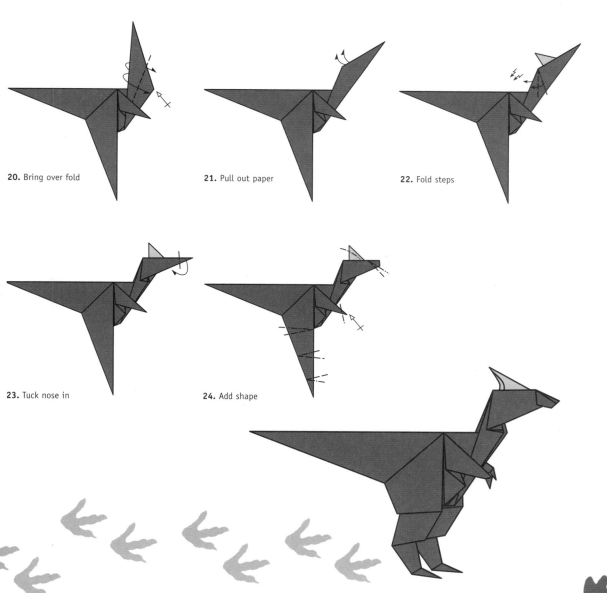

20. Bring over fold

21. Pull out paper

22. Fold steps

23. Tuck nose in

24. Add shape

PARASAUROLOPHUS 41

PREHISTORIC MAN

With his powerful build and broad shoulders, this primitive being spends most of his time making arrowheads and other useful tools, all essential for the survival of his tribe. Hobbies include hunting and foraging.

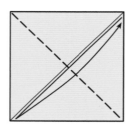

1. Fold and unfold

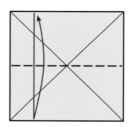

2. Fold and unfold

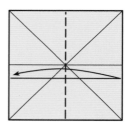

3. Fold and unfold

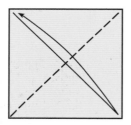

4. Fold and unfold

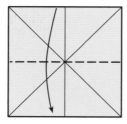

5. Fold in half

6. Push in corners

7. Fold and unfold

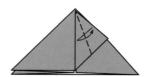

8. Fold and unfold

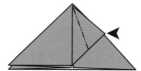

9. Push in section

10. Fold flap

11. Fold and unfold

12. Push in section

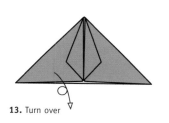

13. Turn over

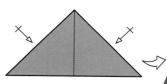

14. Repeat steps 7 to 12

CLASSIFICATION

NAME'S MEANING: Primitive human
DIETARY PREFERENCE: Carnivore
PERIOD: Any
SKILL LEVEL:

PAPER SIZE: 21cm x 21cm
(8¼in x 8¼in)
MODEL SIZE: 11cm (4¼in)

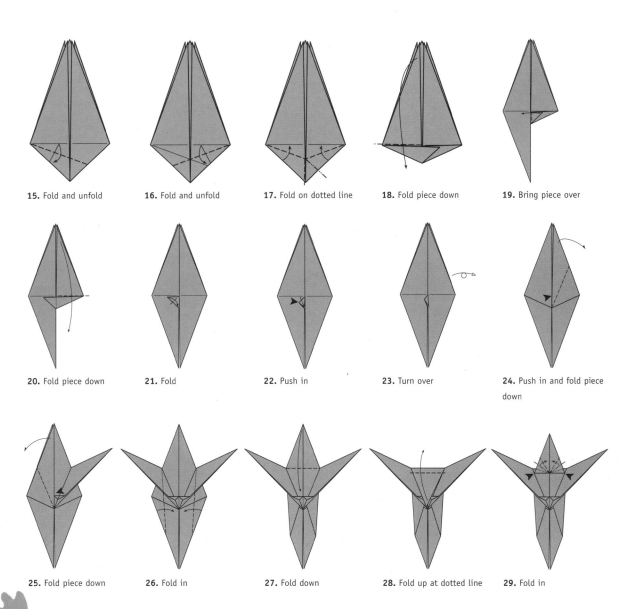

15. Fold and unfold

16. Fold and unfold

17. Fold on dotted line

18. Fold piece down

19. Bring piece over

20. Fold piece down

21. Fold

22. Push in

23. Turn over

24. Push in and fold piece down

25. Fold piece down

26. Fold in

27. Fold down

28. Fold up at dotted line

29. Fold in

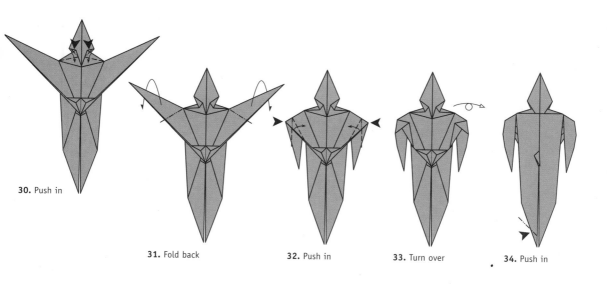

30. Push in

31. Fold back

32. Push in

33. Turn over

34. Push in

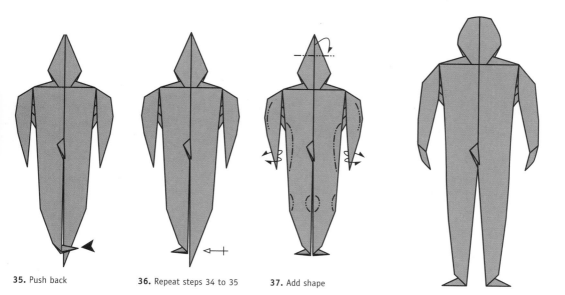

35. Push back

36. Repeat steps 34 to 35

37. Add shape

MAMENCHISAURUS

A cousin of the Diplodocus, this friendly forager enjoys a diet rich in plants – especially conifers, club mosses and ferns. Its long neck and whip-like tail, speckled skin, padded feet and magnificent posture will keep keen dino-enthusiasts on their toes.

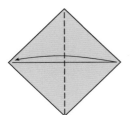

1. Fold and unfold

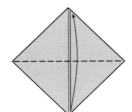

2. Fold and unfold

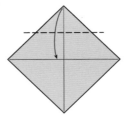

3. Fold piece down

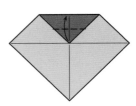

4. Fold piece up

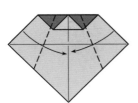

5. Fold sides into centre

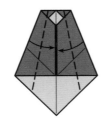

6. Fold sides into centre

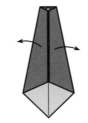

7. Unfold

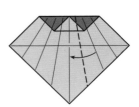

8. Fold on dotted line

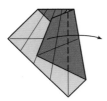

9. Fold on dotted line

10. Fold on dotted line

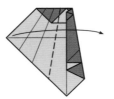

11. Fold on dotted line

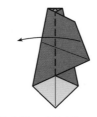

12. Fold on dotted line

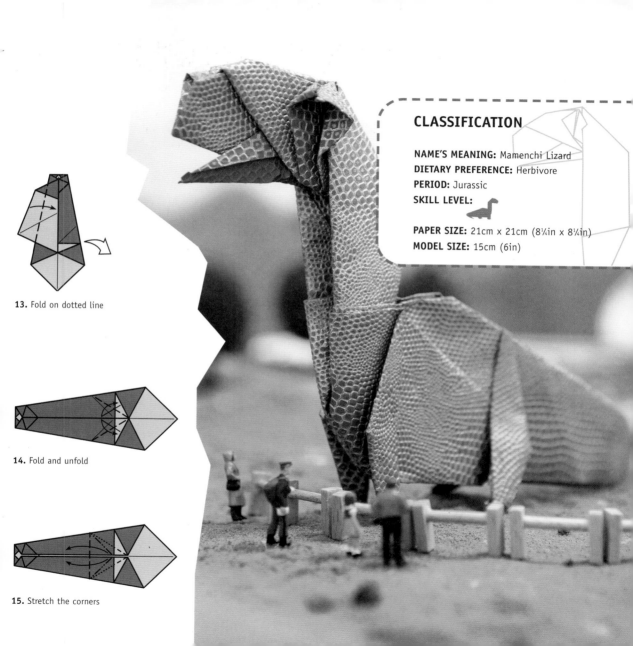

13. Fold on dotted line

14. Fold and unfold

15. Stretch the corners

CLASSIFICATION

NAME'S MEANING: Mamenchi Lizard
DIETARY PREFERENCE: Herbivore
PERIOD: Jurassic
SKILL LEVEL:

PAPER SIZE: 21cm x 21cm (8¼in x 8¼in)
MODEL SIZE: 15cm (6in)

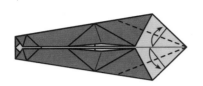

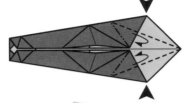

16. Fold and unfold

17. Push in and fold piece over

18. See close-ups in steps 19 to 27

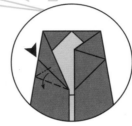

19. Fold and unfold

20. Push in

21. Open and flatten

22. Fold into centre

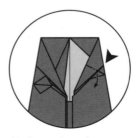

23. Fold and unfold

24. Press in

25. Open and squash

26. Fold into centre

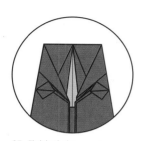

27. Finished view

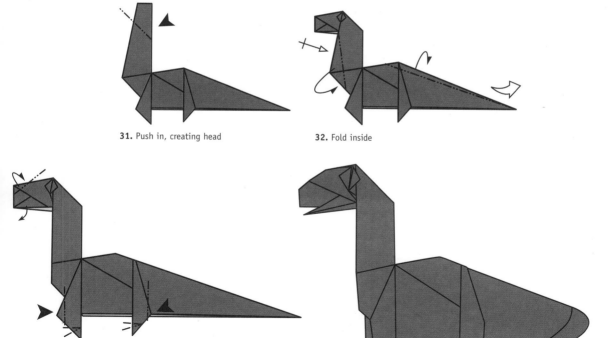

28. Fold in half

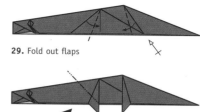

29. Fold out flaps

30. Push in, creating neck

31. Push in, creating head

32. Fold inside

33. Add shape

DIPLODOCUS

Proud to be one of the longest animals to ever live, this easy-going creature is a firm family favourite. Travelling in herds and searching for food; they spend most days plodding the land and eating vast quantities of seasonal greens.

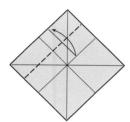

1. Fold and unfold

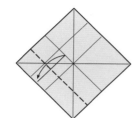

2. Fold and unfold

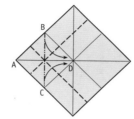

3. Join corners A, B and C with D

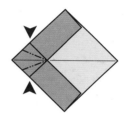

4. Push in

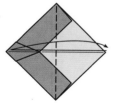

5. Fold and unfold

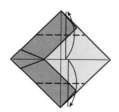

6. Fold and unfold

7. Fold and unfold

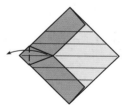

8. Fold piece out

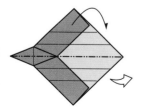

9. Fold in half

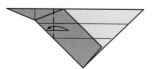

10. Fold and unfold

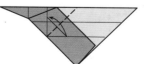

11. Fold and unfold

12. Fold and unfold

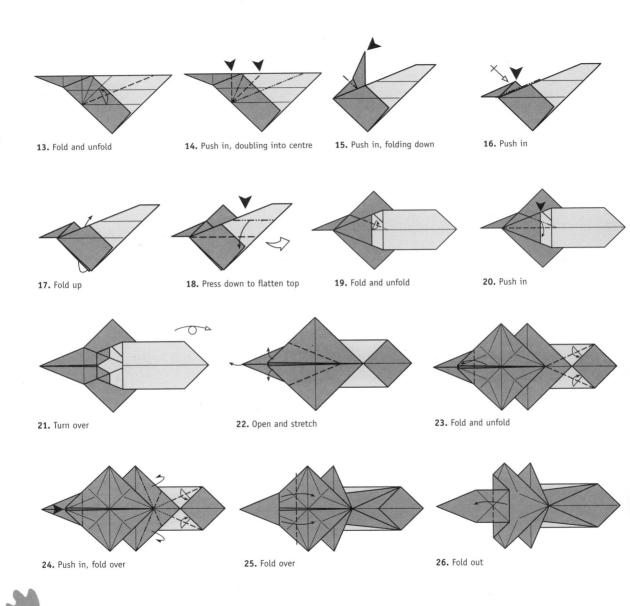

13. Fold and unfold

14. Push in, doubling into centre

15. Push in, folding down

16. Push in

17. Fold up

18. Press down to flatten top

19. Fold and unfold

20. Push in

21. Turn over

22. Open and stretch

23. Fold and unfold

24. Push in, fold over

25. Fold over

26. Fold out

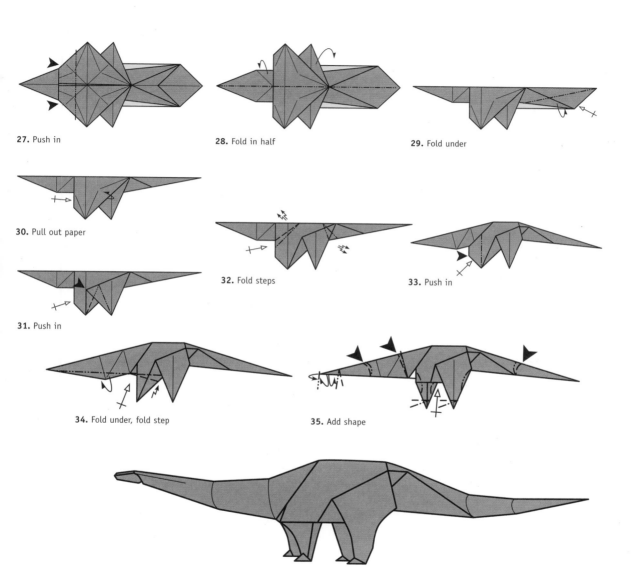

27. Push in

28. Fold in half

29. Fold under

30. Pull out paper

32. Fold steps

33. Push in

31. Push in

34. Fold under, fold step

35. Add shape

CLASSIFICATION

NAME'S MEANING: First Horned Face
DIETARY PREFERENCE: Herbivore
PERIOD: Cretaceous
SKILL LEVEL:

PAPER SIZE: 15cm x 15cm (6in x 6in)
MODEL SIZE: 9cm (3½in)

PROTOCERATOPS

This flirty dinosaur uses its frilly neck and parrot beak to attract other Protoceratops. These horned creatures are known as the sheep of Dinoworld. Hobbies include galloping like a horse and grazing the land.

1. Fold and unfold

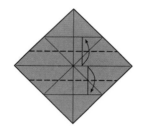

2. Fold and unfold

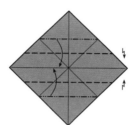

3. Fold in following steps

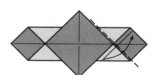

4. Fold and unfold

5. Fold and unfold

6. Fold and unfold

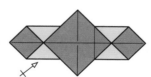

7. Repeat steps 4 to 6 symmetrically

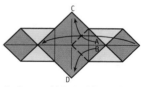

8. Open and join A with C and B with D, fold piece over

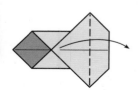

9. Fold out

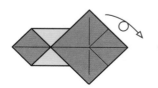

10. Turn over

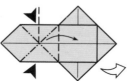

11. Push in and fold in

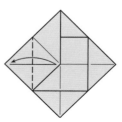

12. Fold and unfold

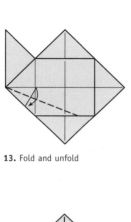

13. Fold and unfold

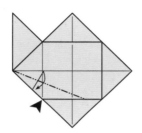

14. Fold and unfold, push in

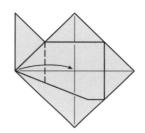

15. Fold in

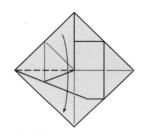

16. Fold over

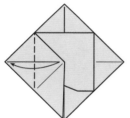

17. Fold out

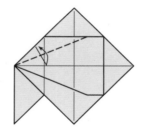

18. Fold and unfold

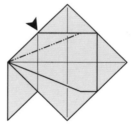

19. Push in

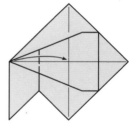

20. Fold in

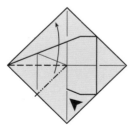

21. Push in and fold up

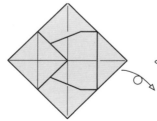

22. Turn over

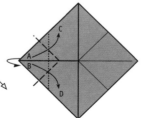

23. Open and join A with C and B with D

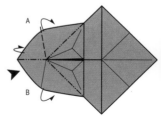

24. Invert folds, pushing A and B towards the back

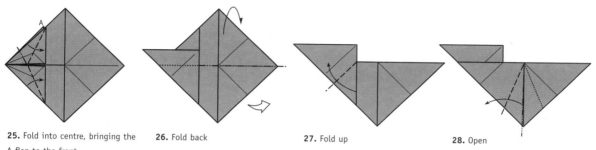

25. Fold into centre, bringing the
A flap to the front

26. Fold back

27. Fold up

28. Open

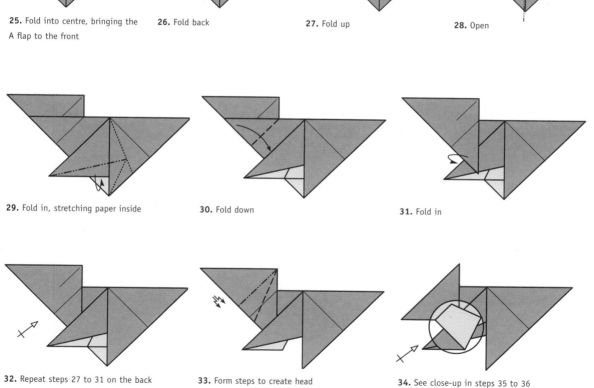

29. Fold in, stretching paper inside

30. Fold down

31. Fold in

32. Repeat steps 27 to 31 on the back

33. Form steps to create head

34. See close-up in steps 35 to 36

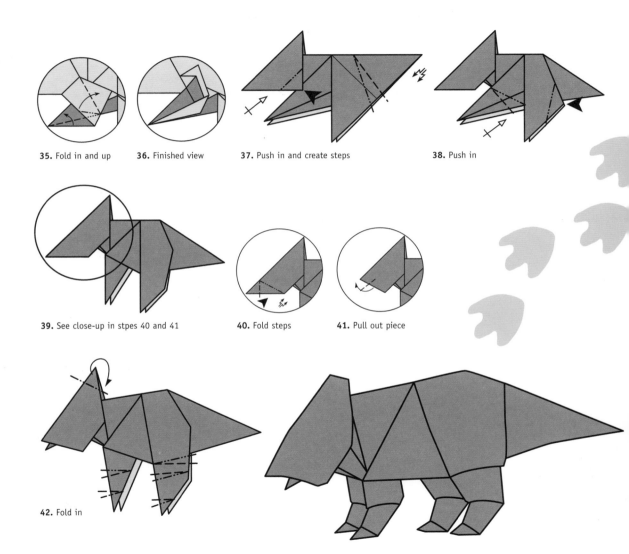

35. Fold in and up

36. Finished view

37. Push in and create steps

38. Push in

39. See close-up in stpes 40 and 41

40. Fold steps

41. Pull out piece

42. Fold in

STEGOSAURUS

Spike, the prickly Stegosaurus, keeps a low profile with his head to the ground but his tail swung high! Bony plates along his spine and a mace-like tail make him a red-hot attraction at this Jurassic Park.

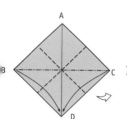

1. Join corners A, B and C with D

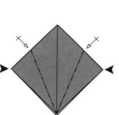

2. Push in

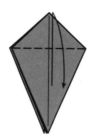

3. Fold and unfold

4. Fold piece up

5. Fold piece down

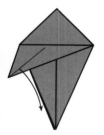

6. Stretch piece down

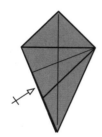

7. Repeat steps 4 to 6

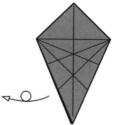

8. Turn over

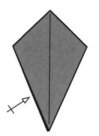

9. Repeat steps 3 to 7

10. See close-ups in steps 11 to 18

11. Fold and unfold

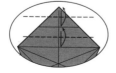

12. Fold and unfold

13. Fold and unfold

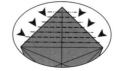

14. Push in the steps

15. Fold and unfold

16. Fold into centre

17. Fold in

18. Repeat steps 15 to 17

CLASSIFICATION

NAME'S MEANING: Plated Lizard
DIETARY PREFERENCE: Herbivore
PERIOD: Jurassic
SKILL LEVEL:

PAPER SIZE: 21cm x 21cm (8¼in x 8¼in)
MODEL SIZE: 12cm (4½in)

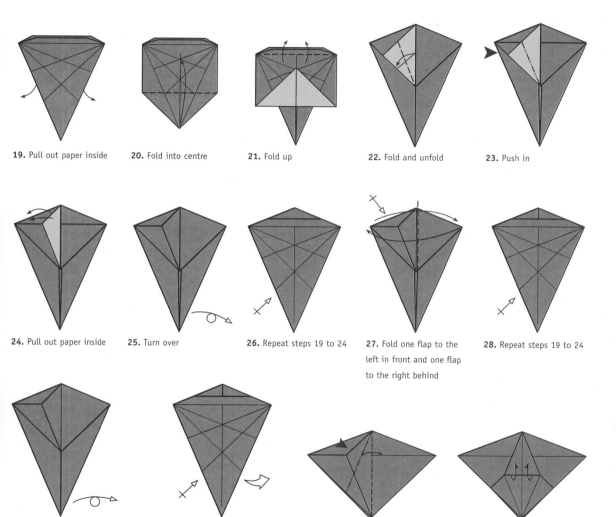

19. Pull out paper inside

20. Fold into centre

21. Fold up

22. Fold and unfold

23. Push in

24. Pull out paper inside

25. Turn over

26. Repeat steps 19 to 24

27. Fold one flap to the left in front and one flap to the right behind

28. Repeat steps 19 to 24

29. Turn over

30. Repeat steps 19 to 24

31. Fold piece over

32. Pull out piece

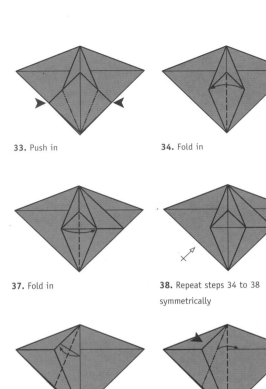

33. Push in

34. Fold in

35. Fold up

36. Fold in

37. Fold in

38. Repeat steps 34 to 38 symmetrically

39. Fold pieces down

40. Turn over

41. Fold and unfold

42. Fold over and push in

43. Pull out piece

44. Push in

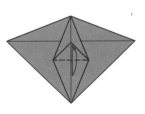

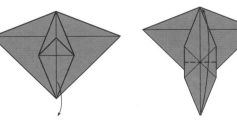

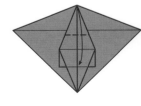

45. Fold and unfold

46. Stretch piece down

47. Fold up

48. Fold down

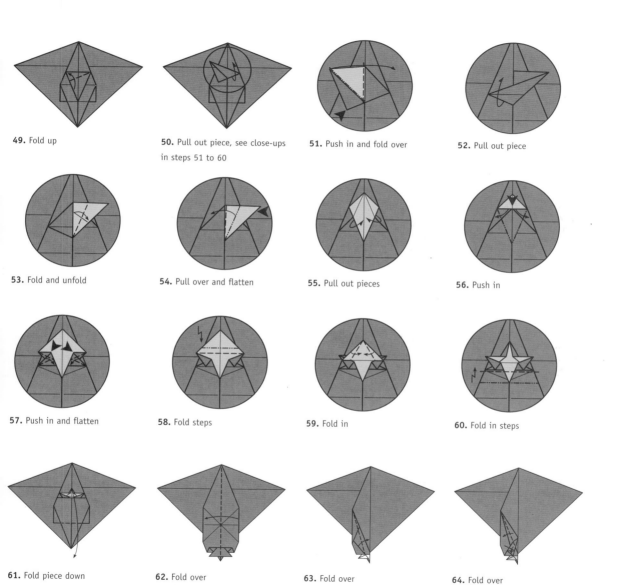

49. Fold up

50. Pull out piece, see close-ups in steps 51 to 60

51. Push in and fold over

52. Pull out piece

53. Fold and unfold

54. Pull over and flatten

55. Pull out pieces

56. Push in

57. Push in and flatten

58. Fold steps

59. Fold in

60. Fold in steps

61. Fold piece down

62. Fold over

63. Fold over

64. Fold over

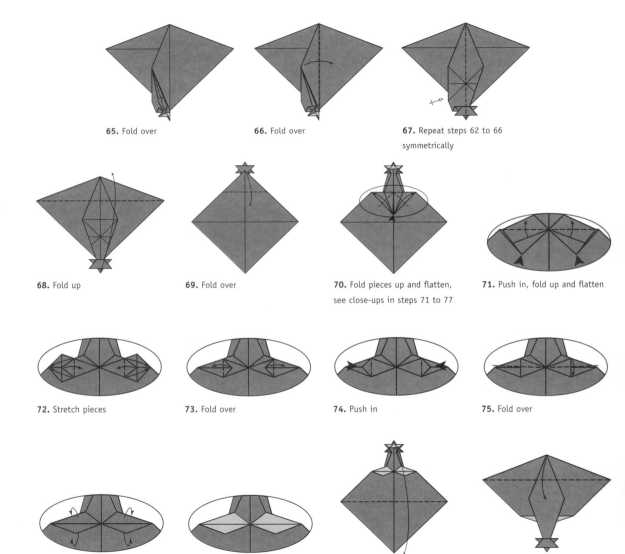

65. Fold over

66. Fold over

67. Repeat steps 62 to 66 symmetrically

68. Fold up

69. Fold over

70. Fold pieces up and flatten, see close-ups in steps 71 to 77

71. Push in, fold up and flatten

72. Stretch pieces

73. Fold over

74. Push in

75. Fold over

76. Fold out pieces of paper to reversing colour

77. Finished detail

78. Fold over

79. Fold over

DINOSAUR ORIGAMI

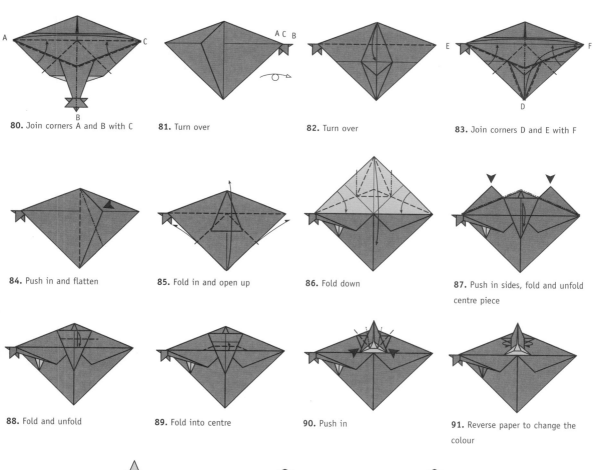

80. Join corners A and B with C

81. Turn over

82. Turn over

83. Join corners D and E with F

84. Push in and flatten

85. Fold in and open up

86. Fold down

87. Push in sides, fold and unfold centre piece

88. Fold and unfold

89. Fold into centre

90. Push in

91. Reverse paper to change the colour

92. Fold into centre

93. Fold over

94. Fold over

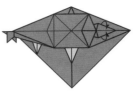

95. Fold pieces in

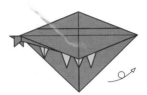

96. Reverse paper to change the colour

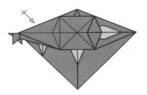

97. Repeat steps 93 to 96 symmetrically

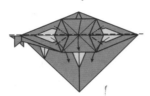

98. Fold pieces down

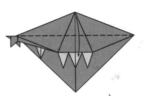

99. Fold into centre

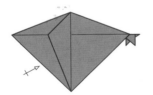

100. Turn over

101. Repeat steps 84 to 99

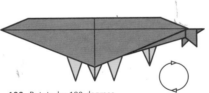

102. Rotate by 180 degrees

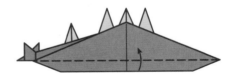

103. Fold into centre

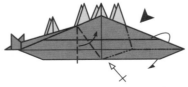

104. Fold into centre

105. Fold piece up, fold back piece over

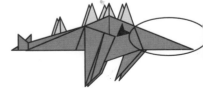

106. Push in, see close-ups in steps 107 to 114

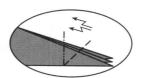

107. Fold in steps

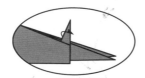

108. Reverse paper to change the colour

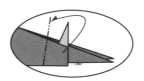

109. Fold in

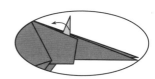

110. Open piece

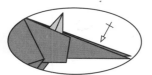

111. Repeat steps 107 to 110

112. Fold piece into centre

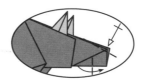

113. Fold piece out

114. Finished detail

115. Add shape

CLASSIFICATION

NAME'S MEANING: Hollow Form
DIETARY PREFERENCE: Carnivore
PERIOD: Triassic
SKILL LEVEL:

PAPER SIZE: 15cm x 15cm (6in x 6in)
MODEL SIZE: 9cm (3½in)

COELOPHYSIS

One of the earliest known dinosaurs, this sprightly hollow-boned character hunted in packs and devoured its prey with razor-edged teeth – most definitely a dinosaur to admire from a distance.

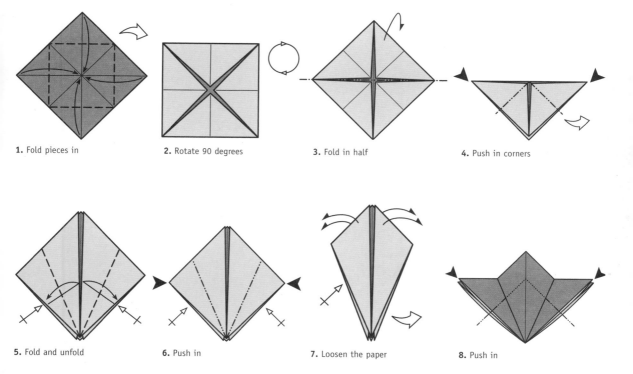

1. Fold pieces in

2. Rotate 90 degrees

3. Fold in half

4. Push in corners

5. Fold and unfold

6. Push in

7. Loosen the paper

8. Push in

9. Push in the four corners

10. Repeat steps 8 to 9

11. Fold and unfold

12. Push in and squash

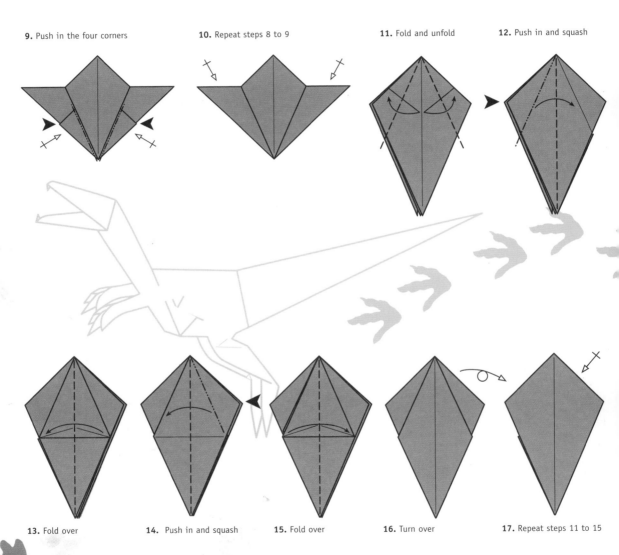

13. Fold over

14. Push in and squash

15. Fold over

16. Turn over

17. Repeat steps 11 to 15

18. Fold one flap to the left in front and one flap to the right behind

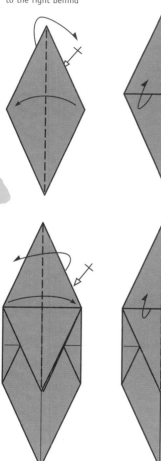

19. Pull out paper

20. Fold and unfold

21. Stretch

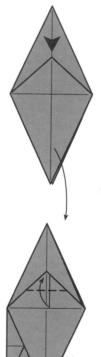

22. Turn over

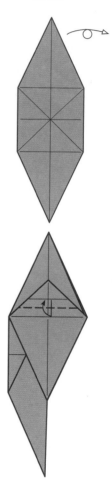

23. Fold in and fold over

24. Pull out paper

25. Fold and unfold

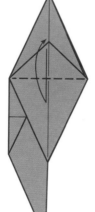

26. Fold and unfold

27. Fold and unfold

28. Press in

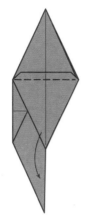

29. Stretch downwards

30. Turn over

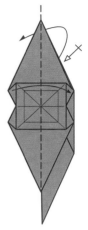

31. Repeat steps 24 to 29

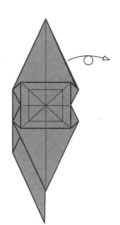

32. Fold two flaps to the right in front and two flaps to the left behind

33. Fold up

34. Fold up

35. Pull out the paper behind these points

36. Pull down

37. Rotate

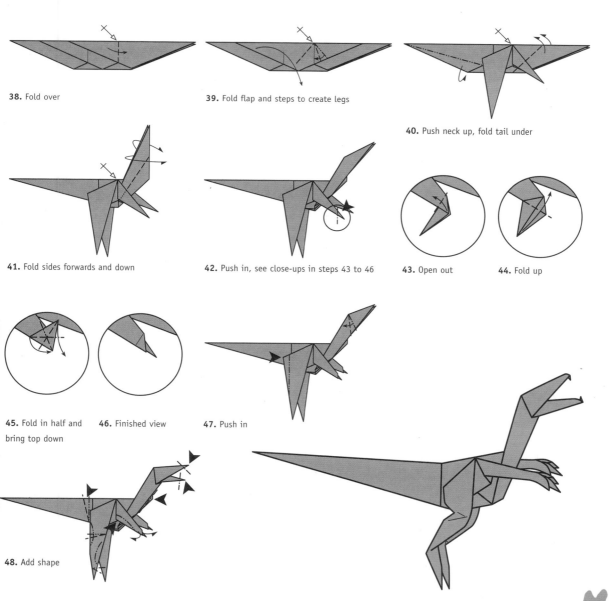

38. Fold over

39. Fold flap and steps to create legs

40. Push neck up, fold tail under

41. Fold sides forwards and down

42. Push in, see close-ups in steps 43 to 46

43. Open out

44. Fold up

45. Fold in half and bring top down

46. Finished view

47. Push in

48. Add shape

CLASSIFICATION

NAME'S MEANING: Stiffened Lizard
DIETARY PREFERENCE: Herbivore
PERIOD: Cretaceous
SKILL LEVEL:

PAPER SIZE: 21cm x 21cm (8¼in x 8¼in)
MODEL SIZE: 11cm (4¼in)

ANKYLOSAURUS

When the going gets tough, this rough diamond has thick leathery skin, a massive bony tail club and heavily-armoured body to protect himself. Hobbies include feasting on low-lying plants and bathing at the watering hole.

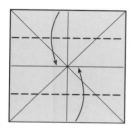

1. Fold into centre

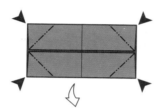

2. Push in

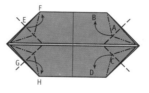

3. Join E with F and G with H, join A with B and C with D

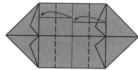

4. Fold and unfold

5. Fold and unfold

6. Fold in half

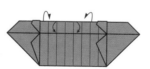

7. Fold into a V-shape, bringing flap towards the front

8. Fold and unfold

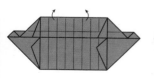

9. Stretch

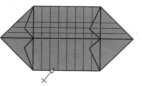

10. Repeat steps 6 to 9 symmetrically

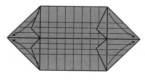

11. Fold out

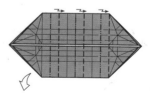

12. Form steps

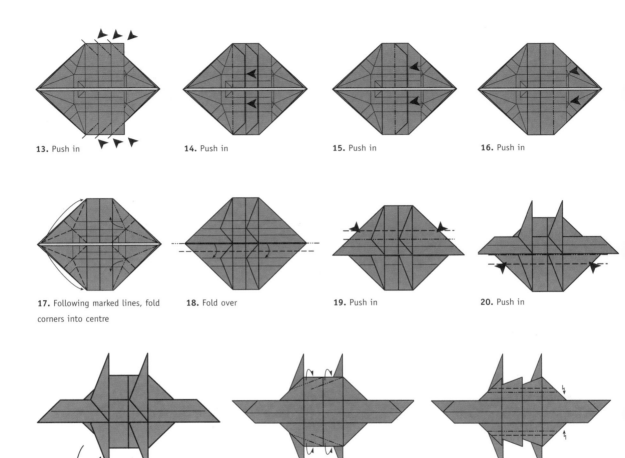

13. Push in

14. Push in

15. Push in

16. Push in

17. Following marked lines, fold corners into centre

18. Fold over

19. Push in

20. Push in

21. Turn over

22. Fold under and in

23. Fold steps

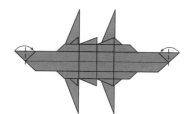

24. Fold in

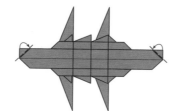

25. Fold under

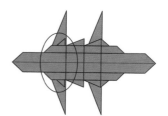

26. See close-ups in steps 27 and 28

27. Pull out the inside corners

28. Finished view

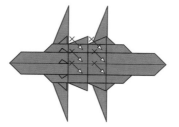

29. Repeat on next 6 corners

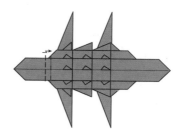

30. Fold steps

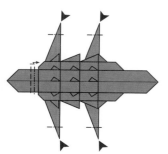

31. Fold steps and feet

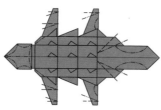

32. Fold steps to add shape

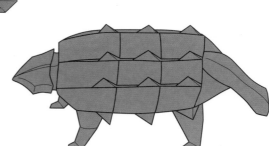

CLASSIFICATION

NAME'S MEANING: Earth Mole
DIETARY PREFERENCE: Herbivore
PERIOD: Cretacaceous
SKILL LEVEL:

PAPER SIZE: 21cm x 21cm (8¼in x 8¼in)
MODEL SIZE: 10cm (4in)

MAMMOTH

A more discerning entry and although not strictly a dinosaur, these prehistoric elephants deserve a place in Dinoworld. Exhibiting lengthy tusks, a fatty hump and intelligence, you'll find them socialising and enjoying group play. Hobbies include tusk jousting and stamping.

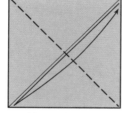

1. Fold and unfold

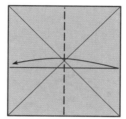

2. Fold and unfold

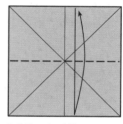

3. Fold and unfold

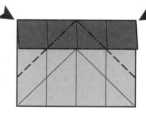

4. Fold and unfold

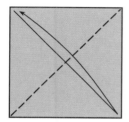

5. Fold and unfold

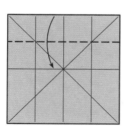

6. Fold in

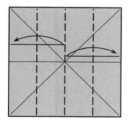

7. Fold and unfold

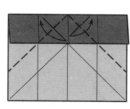

8. Push in to the dotted line

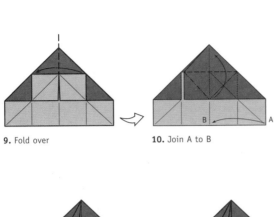

9. Fold over

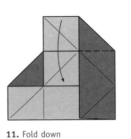

10. Join A to B

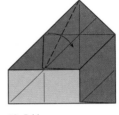

11. Fold down

12. Fold over

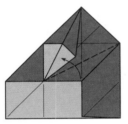

13. Fold up

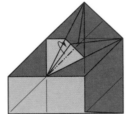

14. Fold towards the inside

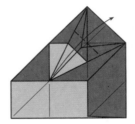

15. Fold up

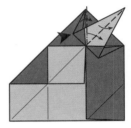

16. Push in and fold over

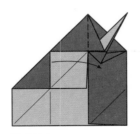

17. Fold across

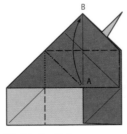

18. Join A with B

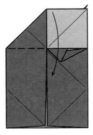

19. Fold down

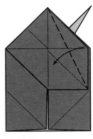

20. Fold over

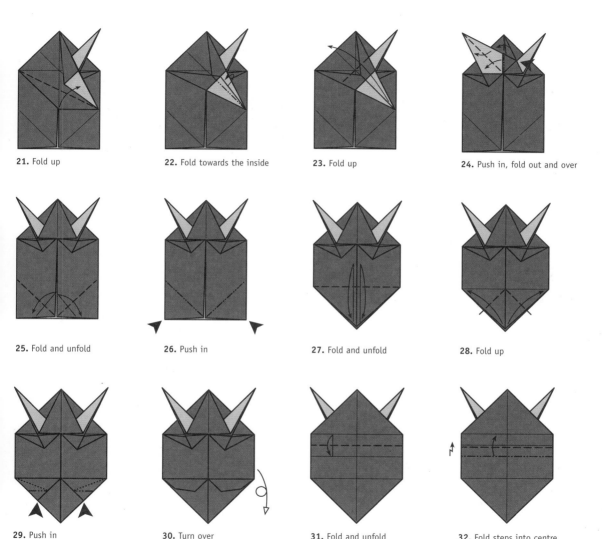

21. Fold up

22. Fold towards the inside

23. Fold up

24. Push in, fold out and over

25. Fold and unfold

26. Push in

27. Fold and unfold

28. Fold up

29. Push in

30. Turn over

31. Fold and unfold

32. Fold steps into centre

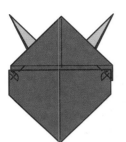 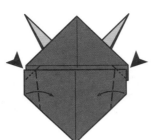  

33. Fold and unfold

34. Push in and squash to the centre

35. Fold in half

36. Rotate 90 degrees

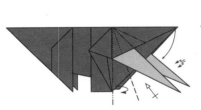 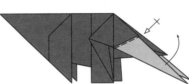 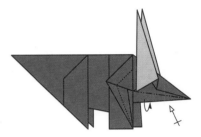

37. Fold steps

38. Fold and lift up

39. Fold inside

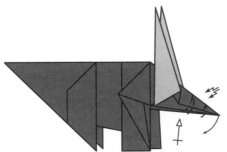 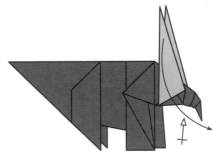

40. Fold in steps to create the nose

41. Pull down

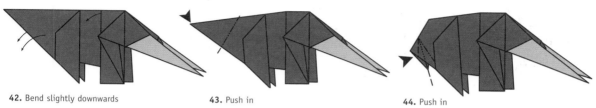

42. Bend slightly downwards

43. Push in

44. Push in

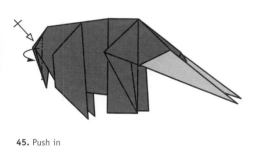

45. Push in

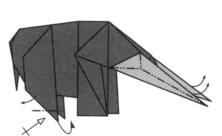

46. Fold in, creating feet. Shape tusks

TYRANNOSAURUS REX

The most fearsome of all dinosaurs terrorized creatures big and small using its replaceable teeth, well developed jaw muscles and clawed toes. With a long thin tail, feet equipped with sharp talons and dagger-like teeth, it's fair to call it the king!

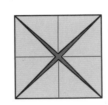

1. Fold corners in

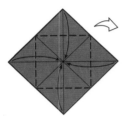

2. Rotate 90 degrees

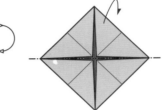

3. Fold back

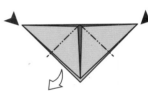

4. Push corners in

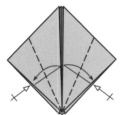

5. Fold and unfold

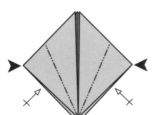

6. Push in

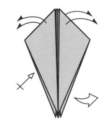

7. Loosen the paper, pull out

8. Push in

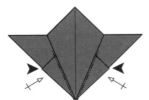

9. Push in the 4 corners

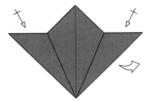

10. Repeat steps 8 to 9

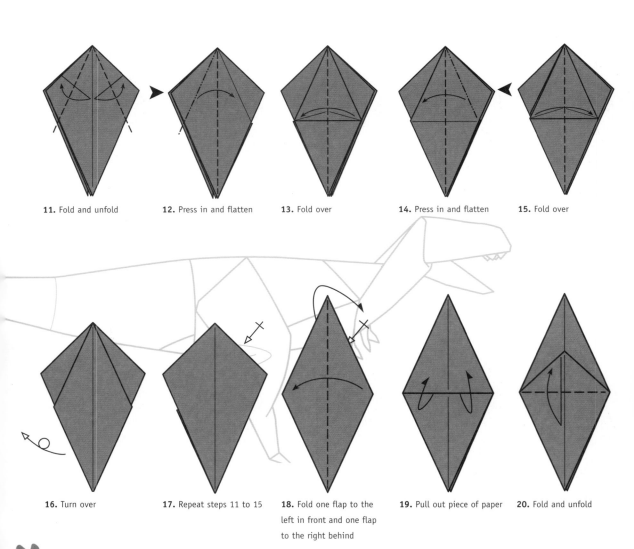

11. Fold and unfold

12. Press in and flatten

13. Fold over

14. Press in and flatten

15. Fold over

16. Turn over

17. Repeat steps 11 to 15

18. Fold one flap to the left in front and one flap to the right behind

19. Pull out piece of paper

20. Fold and unfold

21. Stretch

22. Turn over

23. Repeat steps 19 to 21 symmetrically

24. Fold two flaps to the right in front and two flaps to the left behind

25. Pull out piece of paper

26. Fold and unfold

27. Fold and unfold

28. Fold and unfold

29. Push in

30. Stretch

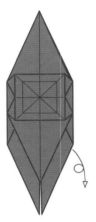  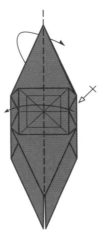  

31. Turn over

32. Repeat steps 25 to 30 symmetrically

33. Fold two flaps to the left in front, and two flaps to the right behind

34. Fold up

35. Fold up

36. Pull out paper

37. Fold down

38. Repeat steps 35 to 37

39. Fold in half

40. Rotate 90 degrees

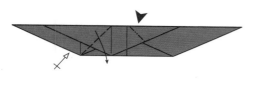

41. Fold back down for legs, fold in and down for front legs

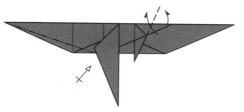

42. Fold over and up for neck, fold in tail

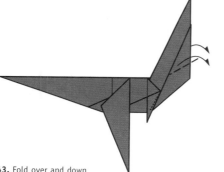

43. Fold over and down

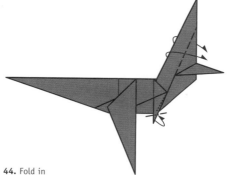

44. Fold in

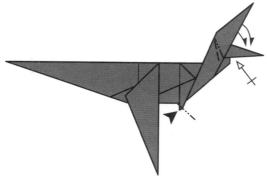

45. Fold steps, pull piece down to create mouth

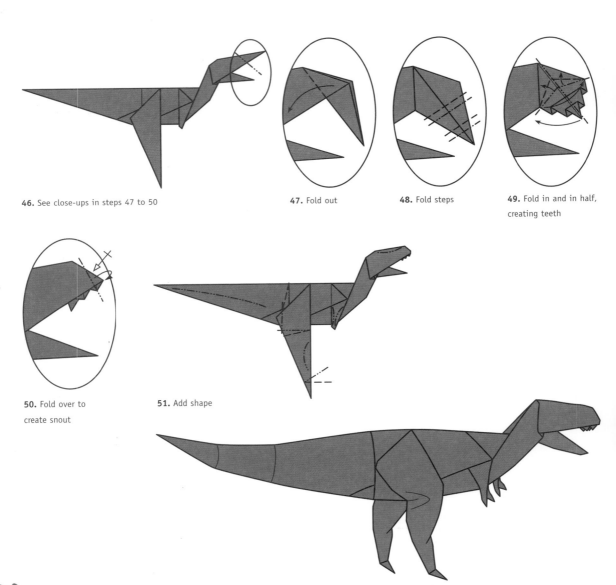

46. See close-ups in steps 47 to 50

47. Fold out

48. Fold steps

49. Fold in and in half, creating teeth

50. Fold over to create snout

51. Add shape

PTERANODON

It's a bird, it's a plane...no, it's a Pteranodon! With impeccable eyesight and a wingspan longer than any known bird, this powerful flying reptile is strong and more than capable of sweeping you off your feet.

1. Fold and unfold

2. Fold and unfold

3. Fold into centre

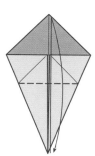

4. Fold and unfold

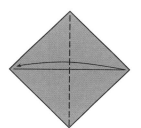

5. Fold up, forming two peaks

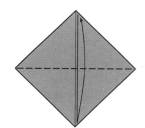

6. See close-ups in steps 7 to 12

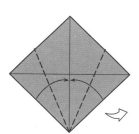

7. Fold and unfold

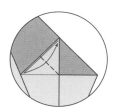

8. Fold and unfold

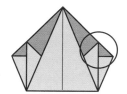

9. Press in and flatten

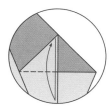

10. Fold over

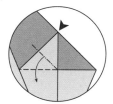

11. Join corners A and B with C

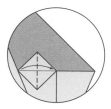

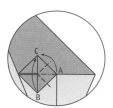

CLASSIFICATION

NAME'S MEANING: Winged and Toothless
DIETARY PREFERENCE: Carnivore
PERIOD: Cretaceous
SKILL LEVEL:

PAPER SIZE: 21cm x 21cm (8¼in x 8¼in)
MODEL SIZE: 16cm (6½in)

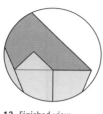

12. Finished view

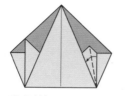

13. Fold in

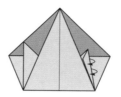

14. Bring out paper behind

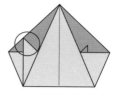

15. See close-ups in steps 16 to 21

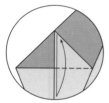

16. Fold and unfold

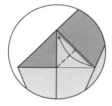

17. Fold and unfold

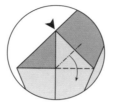

18. Open and flatten

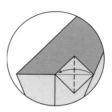

19. Fold over

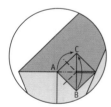

20. Join the corners A and B with C

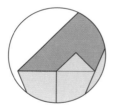

21. Finished view

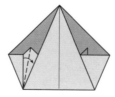

22. Fold in

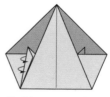

23. Bring out paper behind

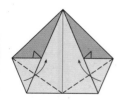

24. Fold into centre

25. Push in

26. Push in

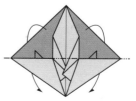

27. Fold back

28. Fold up

29. Fold round, fold bottom up

30. Fold round

31. Fold piece in

32. Fold piece in

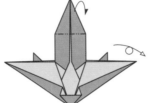

33. Fold back and turn over

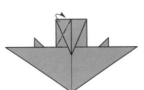

34. Fold piece back

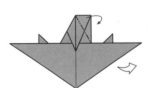

35. Fold piece back

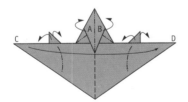

36. Raise the sides A and B, join C and D

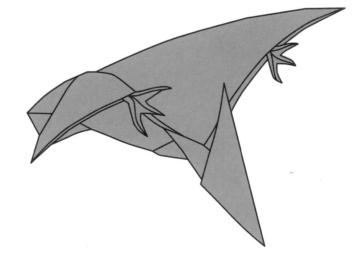

TRICERATOPS

Tri-ed and true! This steely-looking herbivore has a head which is nearly a third of its body size! Sturdy legs, a large bony plate and three horns act as a deterrent to others and if threatened, he'll drop his head and charge!

1. Fold corners in

2. Rotate 90 degrees

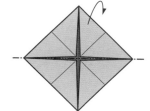

3. Fold back

4. Push corners in

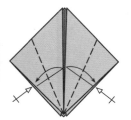

5. Fold and unfold

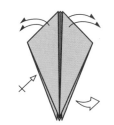

6. Push in

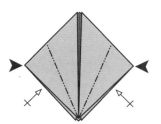

7. Loosen the paper

8. Push in flaps

9. Push in the 4 corners

10. Fold and unfold

11. Press in and squash

12. Fold over

CLASSIFICATION

NAME'S MEANING: Horrible Three-Horned Face
DIETARY PREFERENCE: Herbivore
PERIOD: Cretaceous
SKILL LEVEL:

PAPER SIZE: 50cm x 50cm (20in x 20in)
MODEL SIZE: 20cm (8in)

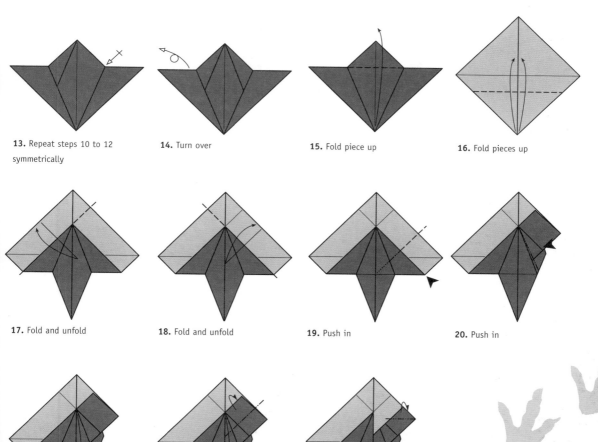

13. Repeat steps 10 to 12 symmetrically

14. Turn over

15. Fold piece up

16. Fold pieces up

17. Fold and unfold

18. Fold and unfold

19. Push in

20. Push in

21. Fold down

22. Fold back

23. Fold back

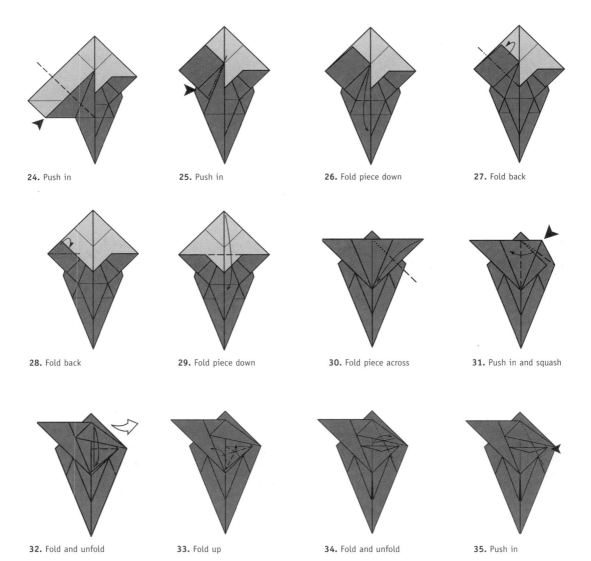

24. Push in

25. Push in

26. Fold piece down

27. Fold back

28. Fold back

29. Fold piece down

30. Fold piece across

31. Push in and squash

32. Fold and unfold

33. Fold up

34. Fold and unfold

35. Push in

36. Fold across (leaving small piece in front)

37. Fold piece across

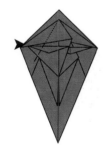  

38. Fold piece down

39. Fold and unfold

40. Fold up

41. Fold and unfold

42. Push in

43. Fold across (leaving small piece in front)

44. Fold across

45. Fold pieces back

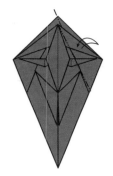

46. Fold and unfold

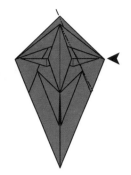

47. Push in

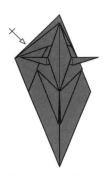

48. Repeat steps 46 to 47 symmetrically

49. See close-ups in steps 50 to 52

50. Fold across

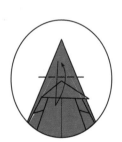

51. Fold and unfold

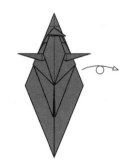

52. Turn over

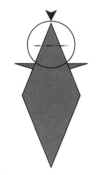

53. Push in. See close-ups in steps 54 to 57

54. Open out

55. Fold edges in

56. Fold up

57. Finished view

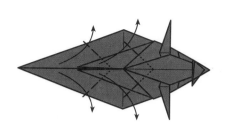

58. Fold pieces out

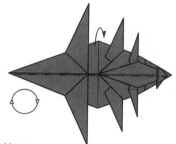

59. Fold over

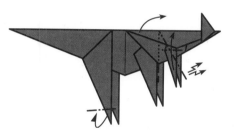

60. Fold steps, lift up section for head

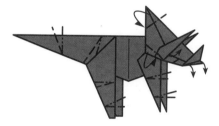

61. Form the feet and the body

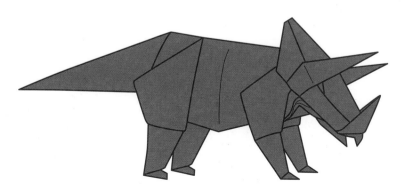

CLASSIFICATION

NAME'S MEANING: Ancient Wing
DIETARY PREFERENCE: Herbivore
PERIOD: Jurassic
SKILL LEVEL:

PAPER SIZE: 50cm x 50cm (20in x 20in)
MODEL SIZE: 22cm (8½in)

ARCHAEOPTERYX

Winged migration, don't let his birdlike façade and wing span fool you: Archaeopteryx preferred leaping and flapping to actual flight. Hobbies include making nests and skydiving and despite his fearsome beak, he's a veggie-loving herbivore.

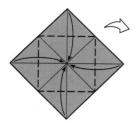

1. Fold corners in

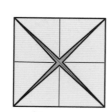

2. Rotate 45 degrees

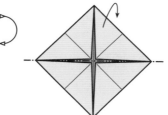

3. Fold back

4. Push corners in

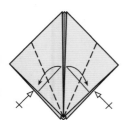

5. Fold and unfold

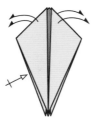

6. Loosen paper

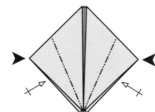

7. Push in

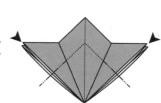

8. Push in

9. Push in the 4 corners

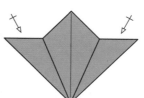

10. Repeat steps 8 to 9

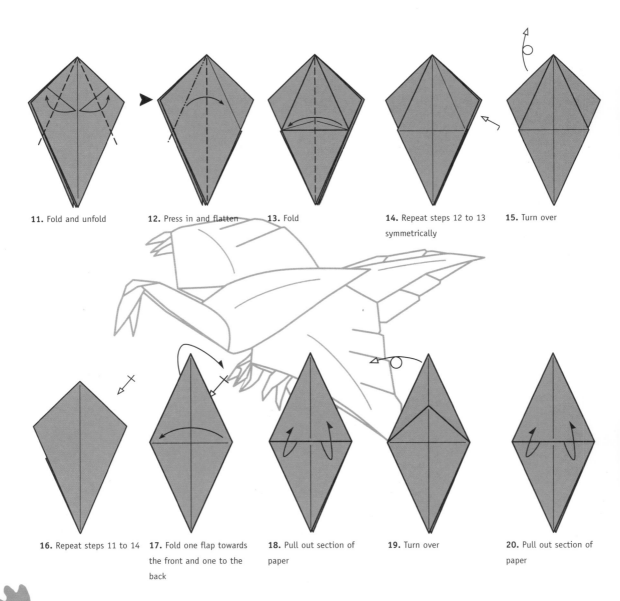

11. Fold and unfold

12. Press in and flatten

13. Fold

14. Repeat steps 12 to 13 symmetrically

15. Turn over

16. Repeat steps 11 to 14

17. Fold one flap towards the front and one to the back

18. Pull out section of paper

19. Turn over

20. Pull out section of paper

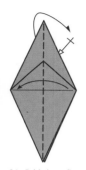 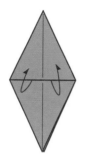 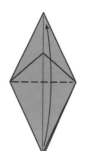 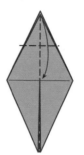 

21. Fold three flaps to the front and three to the back

22. Pull out section of paper

23. Fold up

24. Fold down

25. Fold up

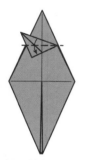  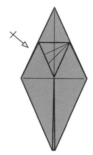  

26. Fold down

27. Stretch paper

28. Repeat steps 25 to 27 symmetrically

29. Pull out section of paper

30. Fold up. See close-up in steps 31 to 37

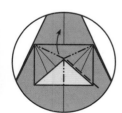 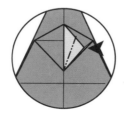  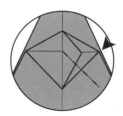

31. Fold up

32. Push in

33. Pull out section of paper

34. Push in

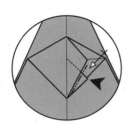 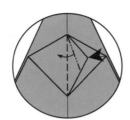 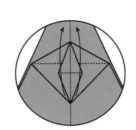 

35. Push in

36. Press in and flatten

37. Fold up

38. Fold down

  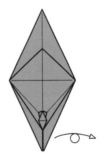 

39. Fold sides under

40. Pull out corner, bringing to front

41. Turn over

42. Repeat steps 22 to 40

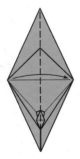 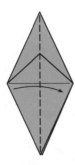  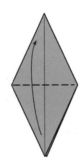 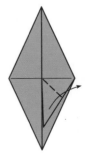

43. Fold over

44. Fold over

45. Fold over

46. Fold up

47. Fold out

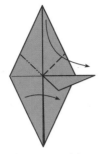 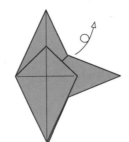 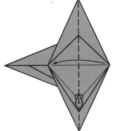 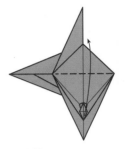

48. Fold piece across and down, fold side over

49. Turn over

50. Fold three flaps over to the left

51. Fold up

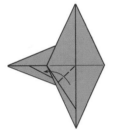 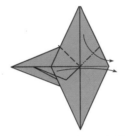 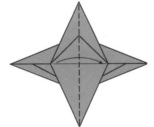 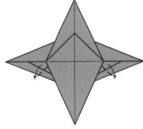

52. Fold across

53. Fold piece down and side across

54. Fold three flaps to the right so that you have the same number of flaps at both sides

55. Fold down

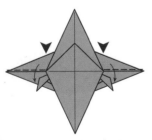 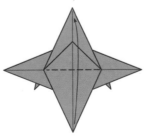 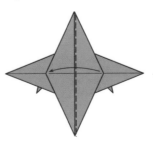 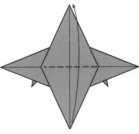

56. Only fold one flap in each wing

57. Fold up

58. Fold two flaps to the left

59. Fold up

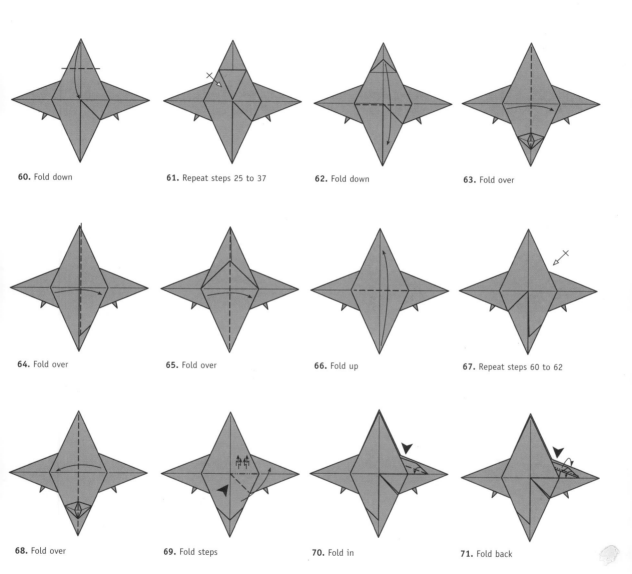

60. Fold down

61. Repeat steps 25 to 37

62. Fold down

63. Fold over

64. Fold over

65. Fold over

66. Fold up

67. Repeat steps 60 to 62

68. Fold over

69. Fold steps

70. Fold in

71. Fold back

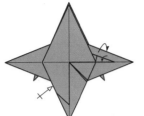

72. Repeat steps 69 to 71 symmetrically

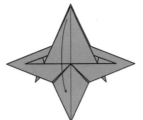

73. Fold down

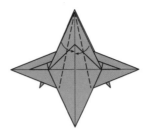

74. Fold sides in

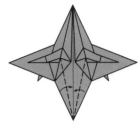

75. Fold into centre

76. Fold back

77. Push in

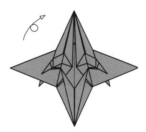

78. Turn over

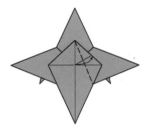

79. Fold and unfold

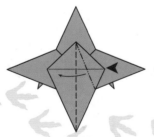

80. Press in and flatten

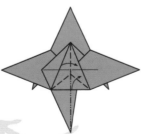

81. Fold across

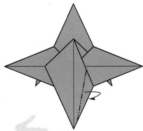

82. Fold under

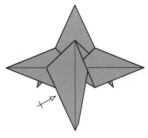

83. Repeat steps 79 to 82 symmetrically

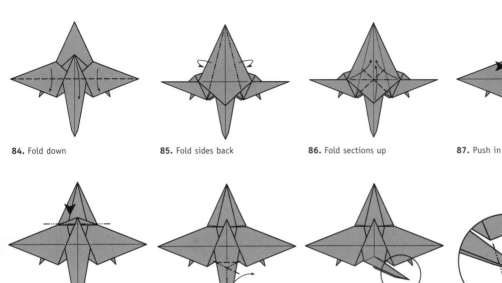

84. Fold down

85. Fold sides back

86. Fold sections up

87. Push in

88. Push in

89. Fold across

90. See close-ups in steps 91 to 93

91. Press in and down

92. Fold out

93. Finished view

94. Add shape

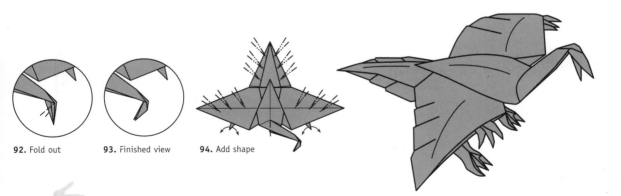

ABOUT THE AUTHOR

Fernando Gilgado Gómez has been folding paper since the age of ten and has since published a number of titles on the subject of origami. In addition, he is a member of the Spanish Association of Origami and hosts his craft workshops around the world.